W9-AFO-472

WITHDRAWN

Human Cartography

HUMAN
CARTOGRAPHY

POEMS BY
JAMES
GURLEY

TRUMAN STATE UNIVERSITY PRESS
NEW ODYSSEY SERIES

New Odyssey Series
Published by Truman State University Press, Kirksville, Missouri 63501
http://tsup.truman.edu

Library of Congress Cataloging-in-Publication Data

Gurley, James.
  Human cartography : poems / by James Gurley.
    p. cm. — (New odyssey series)
  ISBN 1-931112-15-0 (casebound : alk. paper) — ISBN 1-931112-16-9
(pbk.)
  I. Title. II. Series.
  PS3557.U818 H86 2002
  811'.54—dc21
                                                      2002000551

Cover art: "Forms in Blue" by Olivia Parker
Cover design: Teresa Wheeler
Printed by: Thomson-Shore, Dexter, Michigan
Type: ITC Legacy Serif

For Neile

Acknowledgments

Some of the poems in this book originally appeared in:
Arc: "Biophilia"
Event: "Variation on a Theme by Kandinsky"
Fiddlehead: "William Carlos Williams Visits Mesa Verde"
Grain: "Night Moths in the Open Fields" (under the title "Laboratory of the
   Open Fields") and "Five Variations: Seattle"
Litrag: "Voyage of the *Lucky Dragon*"
Luna: "Helen Keller on the Vaudeville Circuit," and "The Life of Objects"
Many Mountains Moving: "Music for the Gods," and "West of New England"
Milestones Review: "Chemical Romance of the Leaf"
Northwest Review: "Tableaux Vivant"
Poet Lore: "Summer Journey Down the Delaware"
Poetry: "Biosophy, An Optimist's Manifesto"
Poetry Newsletter: "The Red Shawl," and "The Nature of Colors"
Poetry Northwest: "The Theory of Transformation," and "Concealing
   Coloration"
Prism International: "A Temporal Bestiary"
Queens Quarterly: "The Beauty of Physics"
Switched-on Gutenberg: "73 Octaves of Nature," and "Field Guide"
H. M. S. Beagle: "The Impossible Task of Ivan Pavlov," "The Nature of Colors,"
   and "The Temple of Science"
Terrain: "The World, or Instability"
"Biophilia," "A Temporal Bestiary," and "The Radius of Metaphor" also
   appeared in the *Pontoon, The Floating Bridge Press Anthology*, 1997.

Poems from this book also appeared in the chapbook *Transformations*
(1995), the chapbook *Radiant Measures* (1999), and in a broadsheet (1992).

I am especially grateful to Washington State's Artist Trust, the Seattle
Arts Commission, and the King County Arts Commission for support during
the period in which many of these poems were written.

I would like to thank my family and friends who gave invaluable encouragement and inspiration over the long evolution of these poems, in particular Neile Graham, John Barton, Harold Rhenisch, Tim Mickleburgh, Blaine Marchand, A. J. Rathbun, Robert Hedin, Robert Neveldine, Charles Cook, John and Shelagh Graham, and Howard and Virginia Gurley. My gratitude also to Olivia Parker for permission to use her photograph on the cover.

Epigraphs: *Songs of the West: Selected Poems of Georg Trakl*, translated by Robert Firmage (1988); *North of Boston*, by Robert Frost (1914); *The Insect World of J. Henri Fabre*, edited by Edwin Way Teale (1981); *The Lost Notebooks of Loren Eiseley*, edited by Kenneth Heuer (1987); and *The World, or Instability*, by Constantine Rafinesque (1836).

The following poems are dedicated: "The Impossible Task of Ivan Pavlov" to Sylvia Skelton, "Household Trust" to Gail Dubrow, "Out Walking" to Robin Skelton, "The Life of Objects" to Neile Graham, "Biophilia" to Jim Clark, "Lady Franklin's Lament" to Shelagh Graham, and "Music For The Gods" to Art Liestman.

In memoriam: Marie Gurley, Richard Hugo, Robin and Sylvia Skelton.

Contents

We die containing a richness of lovers and tribes, tastes we have swallowed, bodies we have plunged into and swum up as if rivers of wisdom, characters we have climbed into as if trees, fears we have hidden in as if caves. I wish for all this to be marked on my body when I am dead. I believe in such cartography—to be marked by nature, not just to label ourselves on a map like the names of rich men and women on buildings. We are communal histories, communal books. We are not owned or monogamous in our tastes or experience. All I desired was to walk upon such an earth that had no maps.

—Michael Ondaatje, *The English Patient*

The land we come to is the land we are.

—John Barton, *Hypothesis*

The Beauty of Physics

Weighing the Planets

—at the Instruments of Science Exhibit, National History
    Museum of Scotland

With one touch I set the heavens
    in motion, on a wire of time
curved within a glass.
    The solar symmetries of our lives

themselves in the turning
    orrery, the orbit gears safely
threading the planets in a whirl
    through an artificial sphere.

Who held these instruments, whose palm
    warmed a polished copper cylinder,
who drew his measure
    with this theodolite in India,

parceling out the wilderness for God
    and Queen? These useless
devices from a ghost-world—
    all that's left of the unconquerable—

now mythical under glass: the sextant,
    the air pump's glass bowl—
there are so many lives' work
    in these tools; how it was to explore

and discover, to subdue the unknown.
    Their stories all but vanished,
the land surveyor hiking up
    a mountain in India

who ignores the ache
　　in his left leg as he hums
a hymn for fortitude—
　　these adventures and the earth

his, with what amazing ease
　　he goes on, mastering
these instruments that are
　　immortal even if our lives are not.

Biophilia

—at the conservation reserve outside London, Ontario,
   after E. O. Wilson

The fox came upon us unexpectedly.
He froze and our world narrowed to a span
meters wide. I heard your words
break into fragments. So uneasy—
something so extraordinary
stood close to where we stood. His diaphragm
rising and falling, eyes searching
for any movement that might
betray us. The smell of water, the directional
bend of a plant stalk
mattered. I turned my head
and he vanished. Melted
into abstract description,
that's just a metaphor for slyness,
malevolence, the implicit threat.
All these qualities he channels
into his ability to stay alert.
Alive. It's nearly dusk; the trees
suffused with dimming light.
We stop by a pond fringed with larch—
rest, still craving a sense
of the mysterious. Your words pour
in and around me, and I want to know the touch
of everything. Described this way,
it's nothing but a glimpse
of one small animal.
Say it's only myth: say he looks
at us from his own world. In the end
it's enough to just believe.

A Temporal Bestiary

Beautiful is the silence of the night.
— Georg Trakl, 1887–1914

We're held by the rhythms of light,
like the fruit bats who fly out to feed

at dusk, rising from the trees
in a gray-brown fury of wings.

Somehow we carry these time signals
through our bloodstream, the body's own

clock predicting that behind our house
tonight fireflies will swarm,

their lunar mating rituals triggered
by the synchrony inside each flash,

each insect seeking the harmony
of others, instinct telling them

just this moment of light is all.

I sit beside you on the damp grass.
It's late, we should be asleep

but a whippoorwill starts up, a dark
portal as his calling grows near.

What we look upon we take into ourselves,
the pollen-drenched blossoms shut

for business; our cat prowls
the flower beds, her curious chattering

at her prey. My trance is broken
by the whirl of moths

around the patio lights,
by your voice as you tell me

office gossip, jokes, that our car
needs a tune-up, how your plans

for the weekend include sleeping in.

What of those creatures like us
who take their bearing from the sun,

emerging at dawn from pupa stage,
cousins of the darkness and light,

birds who migrate to subtle
changes in the seasons?

We are bordered by the earth's
steady pull, cool breezes

so you long for a sweater,
and wonder why we are out here.

The fireflies? The summer night sky?

We walk back to the lit house.
Muffled suburban noises engulf us

until our voices are mere echoes
of what we've seen, satellite headlines

of war. Disaster. Our lives
flare up in these earthbound days,

the early hours when I can't sleep,
can't stop the great curve of light,

its strange powers, its radiance
edging through our bedroom window.

The Nature of Colors

—Isaac Newton, 1672

The sun draws a beam
of light through my room
to the bowl of fruit on the table—
apple, plum, apricot, each
take on a new color.
Thus the visible spectrum
reveals itself

in a perpetual tremor. Every object
shimmers with a halo of atoms
pulsing out into space.
When I pass a prism through the beam
invisible threads untangle
like strands of yarn

shaking out the last flames
of the sun. You have to love colors
to see what's beautiful
in this world, to name them
as they appear

on the screen,
from violet to red; the reflection
opens new mysteries
that the eye brings together,
the spectrum a coherent
language.

Through a series of prisms
and lens, we learn
fundamental truths: how

light falls
from the heavens, conveys
to us a broken image

and we reconstruct
the world, these topsy-turvy
images from our own
blindness,
from what shines forth.

The Radius of Metaphor

A stereo blares country western
two houses away, the world's weariness
distilled to a twangy guitar
that embroiders the baseline.
Briefly transformed by the tempo
I listen to the spaces
music opens and can't close.
The singer who holds onto one note,
his doorway to a place
from which he's been banished.

I tell myself it's intentional,
that the earthworm I dig up in my garden
converts into these words. My knees
bent to damp soil, the circle
I clear, filling a bucket with weeds.
Colorful blossoms, the outlines
of buds and branches,
surge of sunlight
against my back when I—

Here I stop, half dreaming
the girl who wheels her bicycle past me.
She yells for sheer joy I suppose.
I'm thirsty and standing up
tip over the bucket,
tendrils covering my sneakers.

Inside our house, the woman
I've loved these long years—
how easy it is to say.
I walk into the cool half-light.
Her voice as she pours water

into the blue glass I hold.
I lean against the fridge and we talk.
Of my sister's illness, a friend's divorce.

Or maybe it's my hand's slow movement
on her back, lifting up her blouse
and rubbing her spine, easing
whatever tension remains between us.
Shh.... Listen. I close her eyes,
then mine. Are words enough?
What happens next? Daylight fades
on our furniture, sudden quiet.

73 Octaves of Nature

Lying in the center of the MRI machine,
the ceaseless, metallic banging

courses through your blood.

You must remain still; a technician
charts the magnetic current,

the resonant spectrum haloed

on a screen. The resonance flares
through your skin, in your veins

so passionately entered.

The harmonics of shifting electrons
reflect the tenacity of bone and muscle.

Your flesh sketched out

in tones and timbres. The vibrations
map the misshapen pituitary,

the tumor's evidence your doctor calls

benign, some aberrant growth
on your skull's perfect architecture.

These pulses absorb the energy

buried deep inside you, the mystery itself—
how these radio waves, nature's

73 octaves, are almost imperceptible.

We never hear or feel their touch
upon us. A memory or an instinct

to survive. Eyes closed, you see

the image inside your skull,
revealed in the oddly shaded screen.

As fear. As notes that oscillate

between protons and emit signals,
the roar in your ears carried

through the coils and instruments,

where your other self grows
more vivid in a thicket

of frequencies, its music

spreading out over
the landscape of your body.

The Beauty of Physics

—Berenice Abbott, photographer, 1940s

                              In this way the body
                              is transformed to pure motion,
                              a curve away from stillness.
                              The wrench tumbling over itself,
                              thrown into graceful orbit.
Scientists always tell me,
You can't photograph this.
My camera is never good enough
to reveal the attraction
in this universe.
Water droplets that form then fall,
suspension of gravity
visible in their long curls,
in globes breaking apart.
                              While photographing New York
                              I could never keep up with chaos.
                              My obsession: Document.
                              If only the camera could catch
                              the swift surfaces, the city
                              always under construction, skyscrapers,
                              commuters underneath the El,
                              wash strung between tenement rows.
The city always in motion.
Hurrying crowds gathered round me
when I set up my camera,
searching out
that vanishing instant—
that Victorian mansion threatened
by the wrecking ball.
                              I'm not a nice person. That's
                              what I tell those scientists

who say *you'll never show waves
rippling in a tank,*
who laugh at my inventions:
a synchronizing flash—where
balls bounce in precise
measure—a cellophane filter,
camera obscuras in reverse.
I prove them wrong.
My camera illuminates *kinesis,*
a pendulum swinging
on its axis, the slow
unfolding. Truths once
hidden from me—
the structure of soap bubbles,
magnetism and electricity
in steel filings.
Wonders no less miraculous
than Greenwich Village,
the conservation
of mass with the world
unfinished, rushing about,
a city teeming with new visions.

West of New England

I noticed that I missed stars in the west.
                              —Robert Frost, "The Mountain"

—Summer 1912

Suppose Frost seeks his fortune not in London's
literary circles, but in British Columbia.
Say, instead, he heads to the farthest coast,
to find his own wilderness in the slow wheel
of cloud-light, a weather-worn cedar cabin he hews
from wood that yields to his axe's steady measure.
And he grafts himself onto this new country,
its woods, the long unfrequented roads where he's
changed, not the man who spent the last ten years
farming, teaching, the man who set aside his gift—
his salvation in the storied, artless ways of a farmer
laboring his fields. All he can take with him
is this code, his talk that loggers quickly recognize
as their own. The awkward pauses, casual stance,
slouching beside a bow saw like one of Whitman's
roughs, he'll imagine—the trees much larger even
than the myth he makes when he finds a new
play of words, the phrasings of some coastal dialect.
Standing in the quickening wind, Frost falls
in love with the sound a tree makes as it snaps
finally cut free. He acquires a listening air
for this vastness, and steals away from the camp
to the edge of nowhere. He once thought he'd
learned all he needed, returning to the old farm,
about what it means to forswear all but the land
and its people. It was never about them,
their fields and orchards. Here Frost encounters
no one, finds no open land for days, only

the ruins of a native village, bark-stripped trees
carved into ghosts. He feeds on salmonberries,
hardly realizing there's no longer any trail.
Doesn't need one anymore. Doesn't feel thorns
and branches cutting into him, rain loosed
from leaves overhead. Or even hunger much for
idle chatter between chores. He's not going back.
He's made the reckless choice. Those dark trees
admit just a bit of sun, sound of breakers,
leaf-obscured, wind scented by rocks and tides.
There's nowhere he can see himself now except
shipping out to the Queen Charlotte Islands,
a refugee on a beach facing the Pacific.

Chemical Romance of the Leaf

Chlorophyll—a green so common
it's not a color, but a web holding our world
together. Lilacs, roses, the mock orange,
new shoots, appetite ravenous. This chemical
pattern so beautiful, outside on a warm
spring day, pulling off my jacket in the heat.
I wander to the alley. Garbage cans
and junked cars, an old dog who barks at
the cat who taunts it. The kitsch
we live with, building our days around
a breeze in the leaves, their color,
these beliefs we count on, quietly, gratefully—
how else can we learn our lives?

Let me start again. Take this half-filled
sheet, hold it up before me, and look
past its edge at the trees—vertical lines
of black ink blurring to the dark bars of trunks.
This loosening of focus, leaves crackling
in my hands, branches a living maze that stretches
beyond my sight. I stole this invitation
to reverie from the land. My desk
overlooks a small garden, hawthorns and maples
blocking off ugly cement. I ask myself
just how leaves change color,
the burst of light received inside.
I've a beginner's faith in things unseen.

The Temple of Science

— Franciscan Brother Roger Bacon, Oxford, 1278

What magic in the power of herbs,
stones, the heavens, that wisdom
from Adam onward. What magic
in plants, the geometry and color
of rainbows. Only to learn
by experiment, by faith.
To fast on bread and water,
sleep on the rough straw pallet.
Dream of kingfishers
quelling winter storms. Ships
that navigate without oars.
Of what's forbidden me,
the loss of words destroys most.
And I'm denied the sacrament
every day for my hubris,
for petitioning Pope Clement
to end the order's vow of silence.
I'm bound to poverty, denied
books, instruments, ink.
The charge of magic condemns me.
My own works forbidden.
Should I be glad to illuminate a missal?
To salve the wounded or dying?
To subdue the world by the spirit?
In prayer I might find answers
to questions that tempt. Taunt.
How the soul is adorned with virtues—
like a well-polished mirror. Smudged.
Blasphemous alchemy: that science
leads us to the Almighty,
base metals to gold,

ignorance to the tree of knowledge.
I pray his Holiness learns tolerance.
My cell is punishment enough.
Inside it, I build the temple of science,
place here rainbows,
colors that shroud the candle flame,
all things once hidden
now brought together in the
relentless beauty of this world.

Household Trust

An Experiment on a Bird in the Air Pump

—from the painting by Joseph Wright of Derby, 1768

Notice first how the bird's wings curl
against the glass bowl while the lecturer
lifts his hand away and reveals a vacuum.
An easy trick. Those two girls weeping
don't believe their father's whispers about
how perfectly safe it is, no harm at all.

Two lovers off to the side hardly belong,
having stumbled in out of curiosity or just
a chance to be together. A neighbor
attracted by science contemplates the lecturer's
promises of a new universal harmony
for his next experiment. What do they expect?

In lamp-glow and shadows the lecturer stands
with all his machinery before the skeptical husband
whose wife smells of French perfume.
What does it matter if they know the spring,
pressure and weight of air, the ways
a vacuum can create a small hole in our world?

If the bird feels the pressure in its body,
as the lecturer cranks the handle
and the piston inside the cylinder pulls up and down,
conjuring up a void-in-the-void to marvel at?
Some nights the bird doesn't live. On those
he lifts the carcass out like a straw doll,

like the servant's dusting rag, explaining:
nature not science has done this.
Tonight, in the mysterious candle flame

that lights their faces, two young girls
cry while the bird lifts itself and pecks
at the glass. The lecturer uncovers

for us a new truth. With his words,
his hands caress the cork stopper.
The family who pays him sure the bird
has suffocated while he hesitates.
Then he lets the stopper go,
air rushing in to fill the void.

Night Moths in the Open Fields

This is what I wished for,
hoc erat in votis, *a bit of land.*
—J. Henri Fabre, entomologist, 1823–1915

Often at nightfall
I am struck dumb by music,
cicadas glutted
with heat and sun,

the subtleties
of their thorax and lungs
intoning litanies
for Epiera—her spider web a fabric
      of rose-window
night moths are drawn to;

her quivering cordage, impeccable
geometry between a row
of Cyprus trees, where my son
Paul rushes about with a net.
His night-shirt
billows
      like a wildly lavish
thing, white-frocked
with dark wings.
O what discoveries
evening holds. I'm the moth
attracted by lamp
light, its glorious radiance,
a skyline muted by rose
in dusk clouds

blazing down
onto thistle, cyprus and oak.
Science too proceeds by such lantern-
flashes. The small, unnoticed
ones, their habits
and instincts I observe:
while victorious
                    little Paul
dances with his great peacock moth.

I hear the cicadas'
inextinguishable song,
cadence of red earth,
as I stand amid

the patience of web builders
                    who catch night
dew, the unwary moths,
in a weightless
garment of shadow and leaf.

Watcher at the Nest

—Margaret Morse Nice, ornithologist, Interpoint, Ohio, late
   Spring 1933

And though I've no right to hope
for it, beloved 4M returns
one more season, sings his claim
over the giant sycamore.
Sparrows hunt for nesting sites,
flip their wings, a soft noise
when they carry dead grass
to the underbrush
by the maple. By such simple
rituals I am sustained—
the overlooked, the inconsequential
routines of 4M, Uno and Xantippe—
while Marjorie, sweet daughter,
prepares lunch for the other children
I jot down notes
amidst the goldenrod and ragweed.
Here I find the humble beauty
of waste places,
identifying birds by their song.
This same glimpse of the holy
I once had walking along the banks
of the Canadian River
where I dreamt
of the debt I owe birds
for their music. I realized then
how I'd been led astray,
given up on my passion
for this earth. Not by Blaine
or our daughters, but
my own complicity—

and now this disused land
I call Interpoint.
An awakening after my sorrow
over frail Eleanor's death.
Solace for my grief
in the mourning dove, meadowlark
and song sparrow,
their bewildering chorus
as I wait outside
in nesting season. 4M calls
in warning—or invitation—
perched high in the sycamore.
This is our community: its soil,
its weather, the river, the plants, ours;
this is our shared world,
                    our weeded haunts.
                    It's what my daughters teach me,
                    patience, this music too—
                    how it comes unexpectedly,
                    breathing deeply.
                    A sudden rush of wings
                    lifting us.

Helen Keller on the Vaudeville Circuit

—Palace Theatre, New York, 1920

The floorboards vibrate and I
sense from my legs upward their applause—
the audience, the orchestra—for what
miraculous tale they expected,
a child brought in from the wilderness
of her own dark world.

I have no story but myself.
My own release. Teacher
letting water splash through my hands
until the things of this earth
connect with their names:

with the fabric of my dress,
strong perfume of flowers set atop the piano
as Teacher recites our life together.

But the miraculous grows old,
repeated daily for a paying crowd.
Our routine wedged
between tap dancers, trained seals,
acrobats, a comedian so drunk
the audience finishes his jokes.

I place my fingers to Teacher's lips—
listen to her words, and when it's time,
breathe such sounds I can't hear,
the gutturals, labials, vowels and consonants,

that become butterflies,
lilies, roses, our tumbled-down summerhouse,

the sweet jasmine vines
where I found comfort as a child,
eyes wide open in the sunlight.

I am not dumb now. My voice hardly falters.
My swaying body hypnotizes them.
Lost within these words I remember
deep in my blackness,

how we left the well-house
into the odor of mimosa blossoms,
warm dank earth by the Tennessee River.
Teacher walking so close beside me
I scarcely think of myself apart from her.

Household Trust

—Ellen H. Swallow Richards, sanitary chemist and home
economist, 1873

The bell strikes at six. Robert and I
breakfast, on oranges, toast, farina and milk.
Our house lit with flowers and sun.
My morning walk around Jamaica Pond prepares me.
Last night's experiment to transcribe,
another water sample to analyze.

I ask only for longer days. There is so much
left undone. Undernourished and ill-clothed
children die for lack of clean air and food,
our city's water supply contaminated by sewage.
What good is science to them? Or self-rising flour?
Bread powders, glove cleaners? These patented nostrums?

Every housewife must know something of chemistry
for her own defense, how its principles
apply in the home—a spirit of investigation.
Not to be duped by tainted meats
disguised with sauces and French names,
but to know the ingredients and their natures.

For the women students in my lab, the work
denied us before is ours: learning the chemist's
alphabet, among the microscopes, spectroscopes.
The plodding business of Bunsen burners,
flasks and beakers. Male colleagues ask what good
it will do us. The kitchen is our laboratory.

All week I've been in the fields till past nine.
My home, Robert neglected, for what truths
water samples might yield of how water carries
our sickness, our careless dumping of wastes.
When I return home exhausted, I think of that girl
in Dorchester who watched me unpack my portable lab.

The glass bottles, pipettes and tubes drawing her
close, when I whisper, I am a prospector
for pure water. The stream she plays in runs
copper-brown. That's what I tell Robert.
How the girl cups her hands imitating me,
drinks the tainted water before I can stop her.

Runs away laughing, her skirts trailing in the mud.
When I end my story, walking away unnoticed
by the children in the vacant lot, Robert
is already asleep. Fresh night air sweeps down
from a vent in the ceiling. I cover him
with my shawl and see myself in a large kitchen,

a new kind of laboratory. Quotes and slogans
hang on the walls. Menus list the nutritional
value of each food. Outside a crowd waits.
I beckon them to the tables, the bowls
of soup, rice pudding and fresh bread,
offering no sermon, only what will nourish.

The Red Shawl

—Sophia and Heinrich Schliemann on the hill at Troy, 1873

The passage from Homer she once recited
to Heinrich as an invitation for their courtship
means more than myth here in the maze
of trenches dug through this ancient hill.
Each day the burned walls of Troy come into view.
The paved streets and the outlines of houses
laid bare by Turkish workmen.
If only for Heinrich's whisper, Sophia
bends to scrape pebbles and dirt
off a copper vessel they free
from the fortification wall.
Underneath it, gold.

What they share. More than the tenderness
of an old man's love for his young Athenian wife,
how at night they shelter each other, keep
within the room's hushed darkness,
planning how to smuggle this secret out.
For it's theirs. Saved for them
under red ash all these centuries.
Homer's words the only map.

Her body bejeweled, triumphant,
as Heinrich holds her. She is not sure
who he sees, whose image he possesses
with his touch. Or even what
they may find tomorrow, working together
in the excavation uncovering towers and gates,
the citadel of Priam
pulsing beneath layers of stone.

And Sophia, her red shawl
spread over their bed,
laden with these impossible treasures
promises as she did in that Athenian classroom,
her vow hidden in Helen's lament
over the death of Hector,
there is nothing I cannot give you,
nothing we cannot endure.

The Impossible Task of Ivan Pavlov

— Pavlov's country house in Estonia, June 1919

Sarah humors me. Winds the victrola
and Caruso's scratchy aria blooms
in the July heat. What pleasure this is.
My sons play *gorodki*, the wooden snap
of blocks followed by their laughter,
Sarah's shadow stands over me where
I have bent to weed my flower garden.
She offers me tea, its welcome relief
flooding through me like Caruso's tenor,
red geraniums so familiar in my hands
they are an intoxication of memories.
Of the work I promise myself to forget
here, those dogs trussed up, bemused
while I draw bilious pancreatic fluid
from them for experiments some might
call cruel, knowing the dogs will die.
Lately, I've begun to collect butterflies.
Coaxing them with whispers into my net.
Their frail wings, their color patterns
mounted under glass. Slow revelations
of the world's order. That's how I
explain to Sarah my task, breaking
my own vow at our summer cottage
where exhausted from gardening I joke
to Sarah the sky is a blue cerebellum
hoarding its secrets. And cutting deep
into the hidden crypt of the skull
I'm not afraid—wondering from which
nerve among the gray neural fibers
comes love, hunger, or fear?
She laughs at me, at the *gorodki*

ball gone astray by her feet. Sarah
chides me about Lenin's promises
of money, of what we have earned
after years on rations of black bread
and rotten potatoes. Why does she
speak of this, of our son lost
to the revolution? I offer Sarah
flowers I've just clipped, her face
now is the one comfort there is,
the one instinct I know will save me.
To touch her cheekbone, the smooth
ridge above her eyes. And Sarah's
faith. To know where in the body
such emotions arise—this place
of connections in the brain eludes me.
A servant has laid out our lunch,
borscht with fresh fruit for dessert.
I savor each fragrant sliver of beet
on my tongue. I cannot believe how
good it tastes or describe this delight,
the way Sarah cools each spoonful
with her breath and then swallows.

Summer Journey Down the Delaware

—John Burroughs, naturalist, 1878

First I built the boat, a simple affair
    with no center board. Room only
for myself, a few supplies. I felt a delicious
    thirst craving the river, the shallow runs,
spring rivulets leading into open vistas.
    Every bend and eddy testing the virtues
of my craft. Whatever I'd hoped for this voyage,
    I should be home with my new son, not
casting for trout as I float along. This folly
    and excess. Ursula knows our new son's
habits, needs, that love, still unfamiliar to me,
    like the warbler leading her young
down to the riverbank plentiful with insects.
    Their hunger so urgent in song, it's foolish
not to relate them to my life, show what it is
    to me, to the land and its seasons.
In my journal, this seed corn: dry, dreamy August
    days, warm and tranquil, with the shadow
of summer clouds drifting across the water,
    not the noise, the dust, the stench of cities—
but ripples about the bow, the easy pull
    of my muscles. I surprise hawks and kingfishers,
schoolgirls playing along the shore, a fisherman
    alarmed I'll discover his secret spot.
The introspective river, the sky lifts my spirits.
    A solitary heron starts up. Birds
gather in pairs, in small flocks, while I paddle.
    What could be more exquisite? My son
in his cradle, the slow rocking, Ursula's song
    guides us downstream, into evening cool
where I camp, cook my trout, maples and hemlocks

alight with dusk's last glow.
Everything afloat in windy branches
    overhead, the flame and ashes of my days.

William Carlos Williams Visits Mesa Verde

—Spring 1946

Wind-voices in stone walls, abandoned kivas,
      stone dwellings, cliff palaces—

Bill releases a line of breath
      while he talks about
            the breakfast dinner in Cortez,

the old Indian woman walking the highway east—that's
      the direction we all head
Bill tells Floss, thinking of Paris, old friends,

      Ezra ranting at St. Elizabeth's,
      Hitler, the war,
      the international conspiracy

gone to hell. Floss walks ahead oblivious;

these are new places to her,
the snowless ground blossoming.

Are they the first tourists this season,
she wonders, in these cliff palaces (as the brochure says)—

one of the outstanding travel places of America?

The ranger calls these villages hanging
      on the cliff face
swallow's nests

and Bill laughs at how aptly he's caught by the image.

Floss looks through a Balcony House window
              that opens to the abyss below, the other side,
                    and gazes into the canyon
awed by the distance. She halloos across it.

Her voices come back ancient

slowly, out of the long concluding space.
              Bill drifts
in a mild vertigo at this height

hearing Floss among the ruins, remembering
              his own words spoken
                    from the podium last night

the hush at first listening, the poem

reaffirming itself on his tongue
              not a copy of nature
but a dance, words that come
              at odd hours,
                    scribbled down whole

between patients.

Floss hunkers down by the circle
              of stone that once
              enclosed a fire,
and she is to Bill the past come alive.

Above her women dancers raise talismans
      and with each step
         a beautiful measure
protects them as they call down blessings, rain.

While all about Bill are wind-voices,

the dancers.
      Floss and Bill could at least
         talk to one another but don't.

Silence.

Only the poem
      stumbling with their feet
         on the wooden ladders they climb down,

the ranger chattering senselessly
      about a mystery,
the drought that emptied
      this great green mesa
         centuries ago.

But Bill is no longer with him.
His few words recounted later are a perfect memory—

what must be done (a matter of inspiration)
      before the eye, the hand
      becomes unsteady,
the practice (medicine and poetry)
to get it down right:

part of the humdrum day-in, day-out

everyday work.
Because it's there to be written about:

What he thinks of driving down

steep winding canyon roads
            that day, how even across
                        a great distance he hears

the music from their bodies,

how soon he and Floss will be gone
            from these ruins,

not by the gods' signs,

omens of weather or simple doubt,

but because they had friends to meet,
hotel reservations elsewhere.

Out Walking

Suppose we saw ourselves burning
like maples in a golden autumn.
                    —Loren Eiseley

It begins with the bones, our uncertainties
        deep in the marrow. We seek the forest
quiet, stones warmed by afternoon sun—
        the pleasures found in walking
with a sweater wrapped around our hips,
        a breeze casting about the bright,
dying leaves. We name what we find:
        discarded snail shell, wild blackberries
just ripening. A bird up in the trees
        sings his only world, sings
the ferns and salal undergrowth.
        We come out of habit for the rituals
of spirits haunting our earth.
        Aren't they really a parallel life?
A dream, the unconscious? The faulty tale
        of our faith in our own flesh.
Betrayed by our own vigil, we stand
        as a deer noses grass ahead,
the neighbor cat stalks her prey,
        chirping to hypnotize it.
We're sunstruck with these gifts.
        A sudden blazing overcomes us.
What then? There is beauty in cool evenings
        and harvest celebrations, the fall
colors intensified in crisp air. Our late
        happiness has come. Our world,
October at its center, given to us—
        the first chapters in an unfinished life.

The Life of Objects

—Josef Sudek, photographer, Prague, Winter 1946

Against the windowsill Sudek places bread,
a vase with flowers, a stone, a piece of paper;

in others we see only condensation,
a thin gauze over the life in his garden.

The light is lyric. The apple tree
a discourse on optics.

Each day his window is a landscape.
Mystery lies in the shadow areas: a paradox

barely visible in clothesline sheets,
spring leaves unfolding the garden,

or in Prague on a chilly day after a late snowfall.
Under the Occupation a camera in the streets

is suspect and old friends vanish.
What does liberation bring? A new regime.

More shortages. And to Sudek this Jew,
Sonja Bullaty, who returns to Prague

from the camps transformed by the illogic
of war into a woman without a family,

who now believes it's good
to feel at home in the darkroom,

a phonograph playing Janacek's beautiful
panoramas. Perhaps they become lovers,

briefly; their union, their passion
reawakens the city, its horizon

a familiar window—rivers, bridges,
clusters of roofs—in the same way the body is

familiar, even if we don't know why pleasure
beckons, the loved one iridescent in the light,

and shadows between buildings.
If the war, the new regime is undone by

what the body helps us forget, it's a life
found in Sudek's photographs, but where?

In these objects? The ecstasy of his garden
he loves, the apple trees, his home,

his obsession? When I see his photographs
I know how the woman I love is linked

forever to the city we've shared.
Mornings we wake early, sun edging over

the mountain rim to our bed, to where
she unwillingly gives up her body to the day,

stretching into it as into a new dress.
And leaves for work before I do,

noisily descending the stairwell
to the street, the shops opening up

amidst the confusion of commerce and cars—
where I lose sight of her.

The ordinariness of our routine somehow
keeps us together. I don't understand

what drew her to me anymore than Sudek did Sonja.
Or how it can burn up a whole city square

not with light, but the sharp taste of her
in my mouth, the sensual late afternoon

outlining downtown in lush colors,
the taverns, banks, offices, streetcars

in a corridor of light not haze
that swallows us, our house.

Our city so close it seems made
entirely of tenderness and our flesh.

A closeness Sudek must have felt, taking months
or years to print a photograph—believing

only in the spell that overtakes him,
light yielding its secrets so slowly.

The Theory of Transformation

Feel how the vertebrae join the ribs
to form a hollow for breathing,
and how when I place my palm
across your breastbone the membrane
of skin barely conceals what lies
underneath, the sinew and marrow
our bodies are made of—
Consider the webs of bone
in our hands and feet
that mimic the folded wings
of some extinct flightless bird,
the braided muscles now fossilized
channels in rock and shadow
laid down by the head and feathers—
How different are these tubular structures,
how alike, these ancestors
whose origin is proof
the syntax breed into us at birth
is not indistinct or random—
When you trace the bend in my elbow,
the soft cartilage at my knees,
the skein of hair tumbling onto my forehead,
you retrace our evolution,
this architecture of spirit and bone,
the spine, the root of our flesh
where you fit your breath into my breath,
my body into your body—
What we believe, stupefied, in that
blind instant, borne up
by the curve of your lips on my tongue,
the twisting of your leg over mine,
is how this pattern of nerves and veins,
fragile net underneath the skin,

descends from some archaic design—
Suddenly we resurface, baffled
how we are shaped for this passage
by the attitude of the pelvis,
amazed that the bow of my arm fits neatly
against your side, amazed
at this radiant measure lying here,
smoothing each other's skin.

Voyage of the *Lucky Dragon*

On March 1, 1954, while fishing in the area of the Marshall
Islands, the twenty-three sailors aboard the Japanese trawler
Fukuryu Maru (Lucky Dragon) were exposed to fallout from
the nearby American nuclear test, Bravo. Aikichi Kuboyama
was the ship's radioman—

I. THAT FRIDAY: YAIZU

(January 22, 1954)

At eleven, *gun-kan* marches.
Cheers for fair weather
on our new year's voyage.

Well-wishers, wives nearby.
I join them from my radio shed.

Last night's sake still clouds
my head. From our farewell party
where I toasted the dragon.
Our good luck.

Drunk, I sang for the waters
to bring us tuna.
Reliving in my babbling voice
years at sea,
Suzu's picture taped
above the radio speaker,
the tubes and dials glowing
in a starlight
I fall asleep under.

On the pier, now, my children—
Miyako and Yasuko, Sayoko, my young ones!—
clutch brightly colored balloons.
And Suzu, she is here too.
I yell my good-byes—these words
a scarf, a coat,
protection against winter chills.

I thrust my *hachimaki* skyward
like the others. Victory shouts,
praising our crew, our ship.

Good catch and peaceable seas.

We cast off the moorings
accompanied by *Auld Lang Syne*.
Wisecracks about the lonely weeks ahead.

II. THE LUCKY DRAGON, NO. 5

Yoshio Misaki, our fishing master, lied.
We head east to Midway Island—not south.
Head instead to stormy waters.

What if the engine breaks down? What if
there is no tuna?

Last night a squall hit. All below deck.
Only a porthole to gauge if we sail or sink.

Or ride each wake, each
swell, till dawn

when I awaken
bunked by the radio, the sound
of wood giving

yet holding, welcome light,
how it pools and pours,

how it's all around me as I write
in my journal,
this unsent letter home,
                        to Suzu:

I watch the crew take up
hemp lines, inspect and repair the wire leaders
attached to strong steel hooks,

and the rhythm of their fingers
moving through,
                    listen, Suzu,
it's a song
about water. Clear skies.

III. THROWING THE LONG LINES

(February 1954)

Before dawn, nothing on my radio
but reports of other boats, holds laden

with dark, big-eyed tuna Americans prize so.

Soaked in sweat and salt water
the crew unwinds a fifty mile tail for the dragon—

pitching overboard a draped curtain
of baited hooks suspended by glass floats,

avenue of buoys stretching over the horizon—

for what? Our meager harvest?
A dozen fish for every hundred hooks.

I radio this message back to Yaizu: 1,300 lines cut,
searching for remaining 240 sets, cloudy.

The crew grumbling: This is no place to fish!

Why did we come here in the first place?
We'd do better to fish the air.

IV. IN SEARCH OF TUNA

I hook the gramophone up to the loudspeaker.

The crew hauls in coils of floats and wires,
hand over hand to Patti Page, Glenn Miller,
to ease the long hours,

our failure. The hold half empty, they work
the main line as if to scrape the ocean clean of tuna,

only to blame Captain Tsutsui for taking us
to where the fishing is so poor, to where we put out
more in bait than we haul up.

Yamomoto, chief engineer, coaxes the engine
further east, his clothes fouled with diesel fuel.

His humor, like mine, to keep spirits up—
with jokes about mermaids and geishas,

tales the waters give us, of nets so
stretched with tuna we can't lift them in.

V. SUNRISE IN THE WEST

> *About 7,000 square miles of territory downwind [from Bravo]*
> *was so contaminated that survival might have depended upon*
> *prompt evacuation or upon taking shelter. During the actual*
> *test, of course, there were no persons in the area.*
> —Lewis Strauss, Chairman
> Atomic Energy Commission Bravo Report, February 1955

(March 1, 1954)

Nets cast as usual, in darkness.

Lantern light. We drift.
Suzuki, first mate, unable to sleep
stands on deck, dreaming
where the farthest buoy might reach,

sees something he hadn't expected
from the west:
false dawn light blistering
the shadows
with a red glow,
                   a *pika don*,
thunder-flash, moving
over the horizon.

Misaki notes down direction and time,
while we crowd on deck
for the visible
flame rising, changing colors.

As it ascends, spreads
outward, the day sky briefly, a bright glare
in the west.

Afterwards, we eat
bowls of rice and soup,
forget
that dawn from Bikini.

VI. SEA RAINS

(one hour later)

Till a great wind,
above and below.
Followed by two claps. Cannon fire?

Towering clouds billow
up the heavens.
                    What exploded?
Suzuki asks, from his hiding
place below deck.

I laugh, seeing him
silhouetted against the flat
edge of sky
swathed in new cloud layers.

This is no sunrise,
this spiraling

each of us, wondering:
What if the American planes search
for who strays too near
whatever exploded, for us—

the sound of their engines
like a wave over our boat?

Then Misaki gives the orders to
start up the engines,
haul in the lines.

VII. RIDDLE OF THE ASHES

(dawn, the same day)

Morning. Light rain
of white ash everywhere.
In our eyes, in the ropes coiled on board,
my hair, my hands
painted as in a Noh play,

where I'm the messenger, the radioman, who stumbles
onstage bearing his report to Captain Tsutsui:

no sightings of us, only this ash,
thick snow we leave footprints
in—whatever it is.

Could it be salt?

I taste a flake.

So does Sukuki, Takagi. The grit
has no taste, no odor.
A mist and mist spray, that
could be coral dust from Bikini.

Misaki grumbles *that damn dust—*

stings his eyes,
as he supervises the crew
hauling in the last lines for this voyage.

Only nine fish boated today.

The gutted tuna cleaned and frozen—
while ash falls on us,
a snow storm

that's impossible

to escape. Even down in my radio room.
A chalky dew that won't easily
wash off. I scoop some up,
place it in a sack underneath my pillow
for further study.

VIII. We Didn't Know What Happened to Us

*During the course of a routine atomic test in the Marshall
Islands, 23 U.S. personnel and 236 residents were...unexpectedly
exposed to some radiation. There were no burns. All are
reported well. After completion of the atomic tests, they will be
returned to their homes.*
—Atomic Energy Commission, press release March 13, 1954

(on the voyage home)

White dust clings
to our clothes, our bunks,
our chopsticks. Hides in fingernails.
Nowhere that doesn't itch,
though I bathe
myself daily in sea water.

We've no appetite. No energy.
Misaki complains.
His head scrubbed raw, hands too.
No strength when he raises
and lowers the sail.

Yamamoto can hardly read the engine dials.
His eyes clogged with a sticky
yellow discharge. Winchman Masuda too,
wakes ill, his eyes
glued shut, a hard crust
he cracks
with his fingers,
like sleep in his eyes.

Just before midnight Suzuki
vomits overboard,
unable to stand duty;
the crew shares his weariness,

a month at sea, and now
these unrelenting body aches.

From the odd sandstorm at sea?

I scour my books for any clues
of ash at Hiroshima. Nothing useful
about false dawn.

On my radio
static, fishing news.

And in my journal home I write:

Suzu, there is a darkness on my body.
Blacker than any sunburn.
You would hardly recognize me.

Or Kawashima, Masuda. Losing our hair
by mere touch, a hand scratch
brings clumps—something
radioactive in our bodies.
We make a game
of caressing our bald heads.

My appetite's gone, Suzu. There's no
difference between my shadow and my skin.

I don't know what to do, how to
explain the small sores on Yamomoto's
arms, fingers.
                Surely our
illness, lesions, hair falling out,
a nightmare, is atomic,
some hideous aftereffect?

Some secret experiment the Americans
have conducted. On us. I dream,
Suzu, you are here, you wash my body,
heal my doubts—

tell me I guess wrong.

IX. ARRIVAL AT YAIZU

(March 14, 1954)

We enter Yaizu near dawn.
None of the expected
bustle of trawlers unloading, departing,
sailors whistling good-byes
to families, girlfriends, or captains
shouting last minute orders.

A janitor sweeps his station.
Crates of vegetables, machine parts,
tattered colorful streamers.
Nothing but silent reminders of our
departure two months ago.

X. HOMECOMING

Home. *Okaeri-nasai*!, Suzu says,
as she welcomes me,
                    "You must be tired"—
her fingers soothing
over my mud-color arms, my deeper-
than-normal tan.

I realize then how lucky I am,
having only darkened skin, no other

symptoms, yet—
                    Miyako, Yasuko giggle
at my condition, *How dark Daddy is*!
but I don't tell them

how I hid, walking home:
a towel around my face, so that
none of our neighbors might recognize me,
so that strangers wouldn't stare
at who I've become.

Where is my sake, we must celebrate!

Between cupfuls, I am back on
the *Lucky Dragon*, hearing radio weather
forecasts, braggart tales
of fishing boats,

hearing the men above me
pulling in long hooked lines—

for Suzu I
                    encompass those atomic
clouds spiraling
our boat from a distance. The awe
and what it brought us.

XI. TROUBLED DAYS

It's decided. We must find someone
to uncover the riddle of white ash,
sickness
slowly unmaking us.
                    The doctor
only treats our burns with ointments,
a white paste against our darkened

skin. Takes blood samples he proclaims normal.
Tells us he sees nothing serious, everything fine.

Nothing to suggest exposure,
as at Hiroshima, he's heard of nothing
like the rain we describe,
fantastical beast rising from Bikini, what this dragon-
fire spewed forth.

XII. A DIAGNOSIS

(next day)

Captain Tsutsui doesn't believe we are nearly well.
Insists Masuda and Yamomoto take the first train
tomorrow to Tokyo. With a letter
of introduction to visit scientists, a doctor
who has seen such cases before, knows
what heals, the lasting scars of radiation
sickness. Maybe he—, maybe this sunburn, our sores,
our swollen hands, hair falling out, maybe
the Americans, maybe the bomb, who knows what
really happened that morning, a flash like dawn,
but too early for dawn. Maybe this sample
of Bikini ash proves something. Maybe a week
in the hospital, more tests, blood samples,
more ointment. Tell us again what you saw.
Maybe it's too early to say.

XIII. THE STORY BREAKS

JAPANESE FISHERMEN ENCOUNTER
ATOMIC BOMB TEST AT BIKINI—H-BOMB?
> —Yomiuri newspaper headline, March 16, 1954

A reporter has gone to Masuda's room.
Now we're in the headlines:

big news breaking with photographs of the *Lucky Dragon*—
survivors, victims, a national tragedy—
details inside.
                              It's difficult
to work, make necessary repairs.
Men with cameras, scientists and their
Geiger counters roam the decks.

Scientists suited up for a mission to outer space
trace the boat for bits of white ash.
The needle on their machines
a drone, winding its way
into the galley, the cabins,
the storage hold.

A reporter who walked the deck with me
finds his sandals register too. Even the coils
of hemp, this shirt I'm wearing.

Hums. Glows. The whole world
radioactive. Me, the crew, everyone
we've touched— .

Immediate diagnosis: Quarantine the boat.

The fish? Where have we sold them?

XIV. THE CRYING FISH

OUR FISH ARE NOT RADIOACTIVE
                —shop sign, Tokyo Market, March 19, 1954

(Spring 1954)

We brought back: poison.
Not fish. The Geiger counter making
a sound like weeping as it
wands over tuna we caught that day—

a danger we slept next to, inhaled.
Harbor even now inside our bodies.
Malicious spirits, the tuna—
contamination we fear
after it's already

secretly living underneath our skin,
blossoming like an iris
in spring. The headaches, pus,
swelled arms, weakness all over—
until nothing is left
but this malignant humor.

The fish markets closed, for safety.
It's reported even the emperor
has taken fish off his diet.

XV. IN THE HOSPITAL

(Tokyo)

We watch ourselves on television.
Daily reports about white blood cell counts,
downward charts easy to follow.

Masuda and Takashi, being unmarried, worry
low sperm counts mean sterile.
Sores infect us.
                    What is healthful, harmful?
Salves, transfusions and antibiotics, treat
the visible outward symptoms, not those

inside our muscles, our marrow
slowly eaten away. A sadness sweet

as cherry blossoms hangs in the air,
from the open hospital window. Misaki and
Yamomoto play cards, Masuda yells
for his favorite Sumo wrestler on TV—
wins, losses. Anything to occupy our days.

I dream of opening my own sake shop.
More at ease in Tokyo's humidity.
Bright sun and brief rains. The festivals
of spring holidays. *Shobu-no-sekku,*
boys carrying iris leaves through the streets—

and in my letters home to Suzu, I
unroll the *kakemono,*
place beside it a flower arrangement
to honor this season of renewal—
the paper fish, black and red carp, for luck,
for faith in the doctor's treatment,
for my return.

XVI. A DREAM

Asleep, I remember, the doctor pressing
the Geiger counter up to my chest, my body not
my body, Suzu, a cup of sake she offers,
I drink it turns to a bowl of white ashes,

her dark hair flows over the bed, fish!
fish! white sun that blinds me once more, masked
men on board the *Lucky Dragon*, from the radio below
our national anthem, Misaki, Yamomoto laugh,
wheel baskets of fish, engine parts, hooks,
coils of netting past my bed, Yasuko brings dolls
for me to play with, point out where I hurt,
a reporter hovers over me, drunk on sake, my sake,
in my throat a sweetness like apricot, a taste
of white plumes rising, it frightens me, the dark,
big-eyed Geiger counter I tell Yasuko won't hurt
her, it glows in the doctor's hands, his knife
cuts me open, inside is only splintered bone, dust,
shadows and voices, newspaper headlines on atomic
fallout, the crying fish, a black spiral
of wind spinning me, the ship to ground zero,
and I wake in this bed, talking to myself.

XVII. A SCORE OF WHITE PIGEONS

> *Atomic and H-bombs. It is wrong to add*
> *man-made diseases to those we have to treat.*
> —Dr. Kumatori, Tokyo, August 1954

(Fall 1954)

My skin yellowed with jaundice.
Underneath my skin
between bone and muscle
a high tension wire—

even in my dreams
it burns me
with its electricity.

Misaki, Kawashima, Masuda, Captain Tsutsui,
everyone else from our ship, that voyage,
released from the hospital,
healthy. Able now, despite the doctor's worry,
to fish again from Yaizu.

I grow tired, continually poked, prodded.
Blood transfusions to stop
my cells' decay: this radioactive
dosage, strange beast,
can't be reversed, released.
Can't be put back in its bottle, thrown
back into the sea.

Beside me, the sweater I'm knitting for Yasuko.
Half-finished. Red yarn spooled in my lap.

I imagine slipping it over her neck
come winter: sea spray tightens our faces.
We race along the pier, past boats,
their crews ready to leave port,
families waving good-byes.
We pretend to be kites, paper birds
or the sails
on the *Lucky Dragon*.

Exhausted, I read Suzu's letters, how she
works cutting tea leaves in the fields,
takes in sewing to supplement funds
we've had to borrow from the Fishery Union.

Outside a score of white pigeons circles
the rooftops, late autumn trees
like the white plumes of clouds, like
white ash that once spun
me toward sunrise. Toward Suzu
who when I fall asleep

leans over me and touches
a water cup, little boat
to the next world to my lips.

The World, or Instability

Variation on a Theme by Kandinsky

The thunderous clouds are a collision of worlds.
What Kandinsky saw in painting
as each line of the model awakens the same awe
he found in the wild duck's flight, the joining
of leaf and branch, the frog swimming,
the pouch of the pelican.
Slow revelations of our world.
I write these words while outside
the wind, the light, the furious branches
twist in the storm coming ashore,
and what's set free from the heavy-muscled clouds
are opposites no longer held in balance—
above and below, right and left,
the movement and stillness—until the storm abates
in languid and slow clouds, the absence
of movement. I think of Kandinsky improvising
a new composition. Having thrown himself
against the wind's ease he writes: this plane
to the right—centered inwardly is a movement
toward home, to the left—going outward—
is a movement into the distance.
And he raises his brush
over the canvas, over the startling
white world he knew as adventurous,
and somehow an invisible and somber power
moves against the chaos.
This storm and its variations, the cedars
holding firm against gusts that threaten to uproot
everything, how little of it I absorb:
the pigeons that perch under the house's eaves,
pools of water passing cars raise up again,
prisms of rain catching light like drops of color.
My purpose is to find that dark music

the storm brings with it, not as lightning,
but in the branches and trees yielding a path
for disorder in our world
with clues that are everywhere.
Kandinsky painted lines that veered
into the shape of a horse
(the horse bearing the rider with strength and speed)
and into the free linear structure of a picture:
Little Dream In Red.
I make of this crazy weather
a composition of light and dark, moving across
the white field, the wind spiraling
its web of lightning and sound, the curious
arc of clouds blossoming with rain.
The point is always to be moving—constantly
in motion—from point and line to plane.
From this, the experience of color coming out
of the tube, the sensuous tearing
apart as the storm cuts inland and unleashes
itself is a curious world. Meanwhile the brush,
as Kandinsky knew, becomes the branch
outside my window, the cacophony a musical sound,
a hissing of colors, alchemy.

Madame Blanchard Takes to the Air

—Paris, July 9, 1819

A balloon hovers over the gardens at Tivoli.
Over cavalcades of vendors, peep shows, dance bands,

cheap theatrical amusements tying us to ground.
An indifferent pickpocket takes advantage

of the flight's diversion. His nimble fingers
free a carelessly placed purse, the jeweled

bracelet from a lady's wrist as she cranes to
see the sight of the wondrous female aeronaut

ascending to music, smoke veiling the painted
scenes on her hydrogen-filled sphere.

Guide ropes trail like streamers on a child's kite.
A crown of Bengal lights floats below the thrilling,

the fanciful Madame Blanchard, who waves
her customary tricolored flag for the king's blessing,

for an evening celebration. Fireworks.
Its rain of gold cascading outward, amid bursts

of noise. Much applause. We bask in this
nighttime array: sulfur clouds flowering.

Paris vanishes beneath its own joyous hour,
lighthearted revelries, her regalia, the flimsy

cloth balloon from where Madame Blanchard
sets loose a bomb of silver on a parachute.

What can't be seen: underneath the shrouded
spectacle itself has caught fire.

Some valve left open. Or sparks might have ignited.
And she falls like Icarus, thrown free

of her balloon's network of guide wire. The gondola
tumbles onto rooftops over which she once soared,

but that now break her descent to the Rue
de Provence, where gendarmes on horseback

find her. Or so gossips spread it throughout Paris.
About the blackened bricks that broke her fall,

identifiable weeks later by we who mourned her.
Who carried her in a cart back to Tivoli,

crowding around in disbelief, marveling
at the charged air, at her body, *winged-hope*

brought down to street level, made earthly
by soot and blood, bruises settling into her flesh,

by the cloth we wrap her in. By our dismay
at what the sky has given us.

Concealing Coloration

Oh Louis! won't you try once making a background wholly out of the bird's colors: Just his actual color-notes as you paint them.
—Gerald Thayer, letter to Louis Agassiz Fuertes, 1908

Paint this. The plover, its markings, lost
in a spray of twigs and summer leaves.
The white-throated quail dove poised on a fallen
log, the low grasses, ferns, a disguise
my watercolors hardly dare match.
A Wilson's Tern on its nest, the marshy
ground a shadow for the mottled-brown,
dusky and gray costume. Or Scotch Grouse,
hidden among the sage and heather.
When what's demanded, what must be portrayed
is the bird itself. Its coloration.
Out hunting, I bring down a sora, barely visible
in the olive-colored sedge. Paint this.
The bird as in life. Not its skin
stretched and loosely stuffed, as artifice
might pose it on a branch, but in mid-
flight, beak open, wings ajar.
I stroke its feathers, purring, crooning.
Its eyes fast losing what colors might
beat warm as blood, the flush, translucent,

ebbing now. I must memorize it,
quickly. The blur of ink, pigments,
the wingspan, its body emerging
from my brush tip, more motion than substance.
And birds my passion. The frog's view
of a heron, the crouching hare's of an eagle
is not mine. To paint it, though, is
a canvas trick. The background obscure

enough to hide from enemy or prey.
Woodcocks mistaken for the vines
where I spy them. Short-eared owls
nesting on sun-dried grasses, their shading
a perfect match. Their survival depends
on mimicking the changes each season.
I'm a collector of these landscapes, birds.
Working and reworking the jay,
the sparrowhawk, the blue merging with reds,
no distinct line anywhere. Paint this.
A curved surface, shadow of a flower,
the softness in the phoebe's tufted crest.

Tableaux Vivant

—Dorothy and William Wordsworth at the painter George
   Catlin's "Sideshow of Native Americans," Vauxhall Gardens,
   London, Summer 1844

Dorothy and William wander
      Vauxhall Garden's
Rotunda and lawns,
      amused by
the musicians' off-key Handel.
      Only to come upon—
as if by accident—
      the Iowas' campfires:
White Cloud calming his horse,
      Little Wolf
with a bone rattle,
      singing.

They watch Chief Walking Rain
      body adorned
with red streaks, circles,
      a bearclaw necklace,
begin his
      mock assault
on horseback.

Dorothy calls him a hermit
      like the ones
she and William meet
      in a copse of beeches,
where thrushes nest.
      It's as if she's stumbled
into a poem by William.
      Her mind ablaze with headaches—

with the day's
    clouded splendor.

Such energy and confusion!
    she sighs, believing herself
lost—poor mad sister
    who complains to William
of the city's summer heat,
    of how yesterday he left her
to explore London—alone,
    only a nurse for company,
a book, unread
    when at dusk he found her,
confused, chattering
    to no one
at Kensington Market.

William can't cheer Dorothy.
    Or lift her spirits,
when she longs to be
    back among brooks and glens.
He wonders aloud
    about Strutting Pigeon, Fast Dancer,
musing to Dorothy,
    with a laugh:

They look out of place,
    as I feel we must be—
these Indians prancing
    in feathered costumes,
as we gaze
    upon their savage
dances in buffalo robes.

With Dorothy his mood
    glistens,
catching light,

which he proclaims:
An earthly music.
    Breezes sallying
as they do in Grassmere vales.

Aren't the teepees
    a revelation? William asks—
Isn't Catlin's sideshow
    a welcome respite
from London's chaos,
    from our duties here?

But Dorothy doesn't notice
    William's questions,
or the Iowas'
    chanting as they recreate
for the enthralled few
    an aura of life
camped beside
    the fast-flowing Missouri.

Such exuberance!
    William says in praise
to Dorothy, distracted.
    Dorothy who closes her eyes,
says merely, Let us
    go home—

as she holds tightly
    to her dearest
brother William,
    and hears a war cry,
sacred songs
    like the warblers
who haunt thickets,
    fir groves,
in her meadow ranging,

Ambleside's
calm fragrant airs.

·

Lady Franklin's Lament

—after the journal of Sophia Cracroft, Sitka, Alaska, 1870

Another fine day, weather fit for sketching.
I walk with my aunt and our guide, Mr. Belknap,
to the Indian village, the cause of such commotion
last night, incessant drumming, the animallike
cries we heard from every part of the village.
Mr. Belknap announces cheerfully those chants
were no doubt part of a burial ceremony.
Describes how the warriors gathered in one row,
the women in another, swaying side by side,
while the slave was prepared to attend
his chief in death, a rite, we—being Christian—
can never allow. I long to draw the flames
where the body opens to the everlasting.
What my aunt and I follow, seeking Sir John's
relics, the tenuous lifeline of his compass,
a fabric swatch that might or might not be his
jacket, a piece of copper with sextant markings.

We stop by canoes drawn up close to longhouses,
watch women cut halibut into strips that they
hang in the sun, curing the meat for winter,
for harsher times than spring days we've
enjoyed. I watch Mr. Belknap inspect a basket,
cedar-woven. His fingers caress the fragrant wood
as he sighs to explain how the villagers
just won't rest—not until that poor slave
joins his chief. He gestures his final offer
of a small glittering mirror and glass beads
to the native woman. It puzzles me why he

should take such interest in what he claims are
heathen designs. We leave them behind, plunge
into the village chaos, children and dogs.

Life as usual. I pull out my sketchpad.
Copy the chief's house, strange animals painted
across its front, carved totem poles, men
wrapped in blankets, faces streaked red and black—
while my Aunt barges ahead, finds our goal:
the bier of wood onto which the chief's coffin
was laid last night amid the singing and calling
down of animal spirits, gods who protect us
from the forest. She stares at the charred logs
circled by so many footprints even rain can't
erase them, or diminish their power. I ease myself
beside her, as I have always done, constant hope
in her widowed years. We live with the inevitable
despair, the ache, the awful thrall in our search,
which has brought us here to the fort at Sitka.

What will finally set us free? Another sea voyage?
To where I can't imagine. To have Sir John's
body discovered on some snowy hillock?
That we may save him from the Arctic that has
swallowed up so many lives? We share this hunger
for a remnant, a keepsake from his last days.
A journal, perhaps, those letters we've traced here.
Letters my Aunt dreams of. Vanished, or never
existed. Lost to us, insubstantial as bone and cloth
that burns to ash in the brilliance of this pyre.

The World, or Instability

I wish to sing the changeful ample world—
—Constantine S. Rafinesque, botanist and archeologist,
Allegheny Mountains, Kentucky, 1818

Fatigued after a day's walking, Rafinesque feasts
on corn bread and salt pork.
Wasps assail him like the furies
while he eats. He presses new plants,
new species in his notebook.
Later a rival botanist determines
they're European weeds.
Hope is like that.
All is new, new, NEW! and sprung out
of the cataclysms of our Earth.
The forces of plenty abound: the world and all within
mutable, the divine instability;
science. I'm guilty as Rafinesque,
preaching on, not telling you
of his umbrella, a constant companion;
the family he abandoned in Italy. How reading this
you might think him cruel to set sail—
a failure. Like this portrait,
leaving out his later years
in a Philadelphia slum, burdened
with his herbarium, his unsold life's work.
I tell you instead of his wanderings—
his mania for naming: Rafinesque, head bent
down to an oddly shaped leaf,
a small man in a coat of yellow nankeen
stained all over with sap.

Nabokov's Butterflies

*My passions are the most intense known to man, writing and
butterfly hunting.*
                                                —Vladimir Nabokov

—Ashland, Oregon, Summer 1953

Subtle perfume of butterfly wings
    on his fingers—*caress the details,*
the divine details.
    He cuts the thorax. Slips the *blue*
into a little glazed envelope.
    Here it joins thirty other specimens
with date and locale.
    Nabokov returns at night to his unfinished
Lolita. From index cards, sly
    butterfly on the lawn of a rented house,
his American *nymphe* emerges,
    cocoon split open to the seductive world
of chewing gum and bathing suits.
    Nabokov dictates to his wife, Vera,
crumbles each notecard, each clue
    a sinuous trail—*look at those frail wings,*
wild angel—in-jokes about butterflies
    somnolent, settled on an oak log, fixed
by stealth, the green air
    like the long-ago Russian steppes, now
befouled by trailer camps.
    In bewitched and blest mountain forests
Nabokov enters heaven,
    or what might be: scores of butterflies.
Some reveal celestial hues,
    some mealy wings. Such elusive ones

they whirl about the canopy.

    With no other paradise than the benevolent afternoon, they feed on his words.

Field Guide

—for Ted Parker, ornithologist & conservationist, 1953–93

Above the canopy in Ecuador, Ted Parker's Cessna
    flies into a cloud, a mountainside.
The jungle erupts with orchids and birdsong.
    I read his newspaper obituary at breakfast,
while starlings land in my backyard, alight
    on the summer-dried grass vying for seeds,
insects that tempt them to this patch
    of lawn and what it yields. I imagine
Ted Parker patiently coaxing some exotic flycatcher
    out of a thicket: one hand poised over
a tape recorder, the other pointing his microphone
    into the profusion of vines and flowers.

From the stillness of birds he emerges, hiking
    days for a glimpse of an unseen bird as it flies
overhead, reverberant in the gathering moisture,
    as it enlightens the air with song.
He's lulled into a trance while he waits.
    What of his panic? His flight low over the jungle,
scouting out places to rescue before bulldozers
    and backhoes scrape the earth clean for farms.
The canopy so close below the plane's wings
    snag on branches that appear and then disappear,
safely. The photo shows me nothing of
    the opulent country he's fallen into.

No wonder he chose this devotion. A random
    element in that untenable urge to save what
vanishes, a horizon no longer blurring into cities
    or houses like mine. He's given himself
to his task. Low clouds, emptiness, clings to his

body. Which is never enough. For his urgency.
Or the starling who leads an exodus to my neighbor's lawn.
    In a flash of color, of wings. On cue they
descend to cries like their cries. Wind, instinct
    pushes them. Whatever I expect, the birds,
their song—I'm lost between Ted Parker's photo
    and a color-coded map of the earth's last wild places.

Biosophy, an Optimist's Manifesto

*The purpose of life is life itself—and when we have done our
share inwardly, the outer things will follow of themselves.*
         —Goethe, letter to Heinrich Meyer, August 8, 1792

Say it's naive, this belief
in more than Darwin's old manifesto—

combat, the wolf who attacks by instinct,
the struggle of a viper cornering

his prey, our being defined by this way
of knowing the earth. What of that

other possibility, evening,
when our whole body is one sense,

the sky spreading out its liberation
in great splashes of phosphorous,

of the Bible, the prophets,
the oldest poems, the stony shore

of the pond, pebbles underfoot sounding
like a string quartet by Beethoven

in my head, this unabashed
enthusiasm in the capricious loops

and detours we take, eating wild berries,
their succulence a thirst

for the sky, its mackerel clouds,
lit from within, the city

wavering in the distance like the cosmos,
for the owl hidden in the trees,

for barn swallows moving in and out
of our path, in the quiet, love,

where this closeness, this nonsense
takes hold: like joy. These words

a shoreline where we can stand.
Slender ribbons of grass at our shoes

cleanse us, or so we imagine.
We don't know quite where we're going

like the hummingbird in our garden
who searches for the showiest hibiscus

to slake its hunger. Tired, we walk
through damp grass, a country

we explore drawn into this circle
of intimacy by such momentary

peace the body still holds true.
We breathe in its grace,

the night-blooming flowers
another way of knowing the world.

Music for the Gods

— after the Sheridan and Bruce Fahnestock South Sea
   Expedition recordings, Indonesia, 1941

The music enters me, opens me up to a world
where a rooster crows and a gong calls
to the heavens, the Balinese gamelan players

asking that benevolent spirits possess
the masked dancers, their bodies, the glorious
music, a spatial exaltation in each step,

the gift of incense or flowers. Or I only
imagine the temple, the three-ness
interwoven in wooden mallets striking into

the dancer's ecstasy, unexpected shifts in key
as their gods descend. Maybe it's something else
the Fahnestocks capture on their scratchy disks,

the players not aware what the microphone is for.
After his brother died during the war,
Sheridan stored these recordings in his attic.

For him that world vanished with its harmony
or reason, the vast chords that unite us,
where he watches dancers approach as sacred beasts.

What happens to these voices that beautify the land?
The field song, the songs of worship?
This holy fragrance begins with the xylophone,

the long-drawn-out chant of women's voices.
Stays with me in the passion for music itself,
the rhythmic almost involuntary flexing

of my friend Art Liestman's hands testing a new drum
he has made for pitch. Wedging the curved barrel
between his thighs, he hits the flat surface,

and the drum resonates through his body.
Our improvised passage marks a lull in his telling
me how the drum was built, how the wood bound

inside the metal frame adhered to its new shape,
pressing against the looping wire strands.
He plays a random melody. Music rises from

a hollowed-out channel inside the wood, its voice
dark, harmonic. Around us half-finished slats
of wood, the table saw and metal hoops.

All his life he's loved the richness of sounds,
of voices in jazz groups, in women singers,
where the song overcomes a silly broken heart,

even the loss of faith. Neither of us can resist
the drum, our body wholly taken by its summons.
We beat out a passable tune, share how music

enters our bodies no matter what instrument
we choose. That's what the Fahnestocks capture.
Not the Balinese rituals, trance songs, but this

high-pitched world of the gamelan players,
their droning cadences, the steady rhythm
of our blood that goes unnoticed.

The dancers gyrating slowly, but never stopping,
while the Fahnestock brothers give us their
illusion, temple music which the gods inhabit.

Five Variations: Seattle

Begin with this landscape and believe in its sensual breeze (tar, exhaust,
lilac perfume in spring, birdsong rustling through alder and maple,
sunlight falling unevenly sparking
against tall buildings) then surrender to it

the red and yellow tulip blossoms, purple iris
apple blossoms scattering:

piano music, a single note
between pauses and silences rebuilding itself,
a whole structure
                              with the lush grass
and extravagant kites flying above us
abandoned to wind and sky, the park beautiful
with its gauzy tent of trees and dandelions bursting open.

Streets fill with people, wind from off the coast
this day without clouds, a mixture
of leaves fluttering in light and construction dust on sidewalks:
grit, dirt, the choked gutters
edging down towards the prism of Lake
Washington. Sailboats and wind surfers
revel in the chaos, the incongruity
between blue translucent waters and themselves
between what holds them buoyant
                              what threatens
to hold them under if even briefly,
the chance of tragedy coming up for air or not.

No matter how much I believe
in the faint odor of jonquils growing in back gardens
cool springtime air gusting from the Sound—

these occasions are rare
like obsidian or
                            snow leopards at the zoo
pacing in cages, fists of rage
unable to breathe (and I think of the woman who sat
beside their wire mesh cage
imagining she could comfort their wildness,
unaware she was the intrusion
and took their rubbing the fence as affection not
as protection not as staking territory):
                                    the superficial beauties
imprinted on the back of the eye, lasting,
become memory
                    that Beethoven piano movement
every apartment window open, wind in branches
casting their blossoms to air—
becomes for me the memory of music, the pianist's fingers
strolling over the keyboard
                            note falling into note
hand folding over hand.

Music is everywhere
in the players at a Mariner's game, panhandlers on Pine Street
joggers on the running path around Greenlake,
each a whole life in present tense
snapshot fashion where the details sharpen:

street musicians outside a coffee shop,
elbows bent backward
drawing breath for Vivaldi,
                            the crowd they gather

sip decaf and watch,
some lose themselves to the *Four Seasons*
the bright colors in their clothes
counterpoint
                    to Hmong tapestries and pottery,
flowers and crafts for sale or the music itself
midafternoon, everyone moving.

Intoxication of spring blossoms, tactile
and technical: how my senses confuse the pleasure
after months of dull rain, then this bursting forth,
gardens renewed—
                    what was planned in winter
realized, yellow, violet, red
                    colors pulled from the ground
the cord from the center of the world:

not a question of revelation
or even Seattle
but rain-shore with a mythology of mists and shadows
and the long grass at Discovery Park;

where the Olympics
grow silver with light at the skyline.

From someone's tinny radio a sax
gives light and its beauty back to us,
because music
holds plenty of spaces like this,
                    places we create
out of where we live, that stay with us
in the brief exultation of flowers and sun—

this random music
floating out over Shilshole Bay.

Notes

"West of New England" is based upon the poet Robert Frost's decision in 1912 to finally leave his New Hampshire farm and either transplant his family to Vancouver B.C., where he had friends, or to cross the ocean and seek literary fame in England (the alternative strongly favored by his wife, Elinor). This poem imagines the future not taken.

The "Beauty of Physics": Berenice Abbott was the first photographer to capture in a visual form basic physical laws, such as magnetism or gravity. In the 1930s she documented the changing face of New York City. In the 1940s and 1950s she worked alone, inventing many of the devices she needed to capture these phenomena.

The "Red Shawl": Sophia Schliemann was the second wife of Heinrich Schliemann, the archeologist who discovered the site of Homer's Troy. Well into his fifties, Heinrich decided to pursue his lifelong goal of finding this legendary city, using only Homer's words as his guide. A biography of their lives, *One Passion, Two Lives*, describes their first meeting in a Greek classroom, where Sophia recites aloud to her fellow students Helen's lament over the death of Hector. Hearing these words, Heinrich believed he had found his soulmate, and he married Sophia, then an eighteen-year-old Greek schoolgirl. Together they set out for Turkey and began excavating.

"Watcher at the Nest": Margaret Morse Nice was an amateur ornithologist and the first to make a comprehensive study of the common song sparrow. Her experiences and observation are recorded in her book from which this poem draws its title.

"The Life of Objects": During the Nazi occupation, Czechoslovakia's most gifted photographer, Josef Sudek, began a photographic study of his backyard garden seen through his window. After the war, he took on an assistant, Sonja Bullaty, a concentration camp survivor. Bullaty later left Europe for America and became a champion of Sudek's work. Sudek's obsession was to capture the beauty of his beloved Prague.

"Voyage of the *Lucky Dragon*": Aikichi Kuboyama died on September 23, 1954, from exposure to radioactive ash. This account of his journey is based primarily on the book *The Voyage of the Lucky Dragon: The True Story of the Japanese Fishermen Who Were the First Victims of the H-Bomb* (1958), by atomic scientist Ralph E. Lapp. Several section titles and images are taken directly from paintings and line drawings made by Ben Shahn, who illustrated the account of Kuboyama's life in *Kuboyama and the Saga of the Lucky Dragon* (1965).

"Tableau Vivant" is an imagined scenario which brings together several unrelated historical events and characters. While no evidence exists that Dorothy and William Wordsworth actually witnessed George Catlin's exhibition, it is not impossible that given their keen devotion to nature they might have been drawn to this display.

"The World, or Instability": Now largely forgotten, Constantine Rafinesque was an Italian botanist who immigrated to America as a young man. Leaving behind his family in Europe, he explored the new country in hopes of discovering a vast number of species. Unfortunately, his enthusiastic finds were often discredited. Throughout his life he was a voluminous writer and his work foreshadows in part the notion of adaptation in nature later crucial to Darwin. Rafinesque also composed a three-hundred-page poem in which he tried to explain the philosophical and scientific basis for his theories on the mutability of species.

About the Author

James Gurley has published two poetry chapbooks, *Radiant Measures,* and *Transformations.* His poems have appeared in numerous anthologies and journals, including *Crab Orchard Review, Indiana Review, Many Mountains Moving,* and *Poetry.* He is the recipient of various writing grants, most recently a 2001 literary fellowship from Artist Trust/Washington State Arts Commission. He lives in Seattle.